History's Hotshots

Pirates!
Bold and Brutal Rebels

Elsie Olson

Checkerboard Library

An Imprint of Abdo Publishing
abdopublishing.com

abdopublishing.com

Printed in the United States of America, North Mankato, Minnesota
102017
012018

 THIS BOOK CONTAINS
RECYCLED MATERIALS

Design: Kelly Doudna, Mighty Media, Inc.
Production: Mighty Media, Inc.
Editor: Jessie Alkire
Cover Photograph: Shutterstock
Design Elements: Shutterstock
Interior Photographs: Alamy, pp. 9, 19, 23, 25; iStockphoto; pp. 6, 8 (top), 13, 17, 29; Mighty Media, Inc.,
pp. 7, 21; Shutterstock, pp. 1, 4-5, 7, 20, 21; Wikimedia Commons, 8 (middle), 8 (bottom), 11, 14, 27

Publisher's Cataloging-in-Publication Data

Names: Olson, Elsie, author.
Title: Pirates! bold and brutal rebels / by Elsie Olson.
Other titles: Bold and brutal rebels
Description: Minneapolis, Minnesota : Abdo Publishing, 2018. | Series: History's hotshots |
     Includes online resources and index.
Identifiers: LCCN 2017944053 | ISBN 9781532112737 (lib.bdg.) | ISBN 9781532150456 (ebook)
Subjects: LCSH: Pirates--Juvenile literature. | Buccaneers--Juvenile literature. |
     Pirates--History--Juvenile literature.
Classification: DDC 972.903--dc23
LC record available at https://lccn.loc.gov/2017944053

Contents

HOIST the JOLLY ROGER!

It's another hot day in the Caribbean. You've been at sea for weeks. You've eaten nothing but spoiled meat and bug-**infested** crackers. You sleep alongside many other men below deck.

But you don't mind the tough conditions. You have more freedom on this ship than you would on shore. You trust your captain. You even helped elect him! Someday, you might be captain of your own ship. But that day is a long way off.

Suddenly, a fellow crewmember spots a merchant ship! The captain gives the order to follow the ship and **hoist** the Jolly Roger, the ship's flag. The black skull-and-crossbones flag flies in the breeze. The merchant ship tries to turn around. But you know the ship is no match for your swift vessel. If you're lucky, your crew will capture the ship without a fight. You know most of the merchant ship crew won't be willing to die to protect their cargo. Some might even join your crew! However, if you do need to fight, you are ready. You are well-armed and surrounded by some of the fiercest fighters on the Caribbean Sea. You are a pirate!

Who Were Pirates?

Pirates were **outlaws** who traveled by ship to attack other ships' crews and settlements. Pirates didn't sail for any specific government or country. Instead, pirate crews were made of individuals who were out to get rich themselves.

Pirates attacked merchant ships, stole these ships and their goods, and shared the profits amongst themselves. Pirates followed the command of a captain. But pirate captains were only successful when they had the support of their crew. Pirate ships were **democracies**, and everyone had a say.

Piracy has likely been around since ancient times, or as long as ships have been transporting goods. The first recorded acts of piracy occurred in the Mediterranean Sea more than 3,000 years ago. Pirates still operate in

In the Golden Age of Piracy, pirates faced battles, storms, disease, and poverty on the high seas.

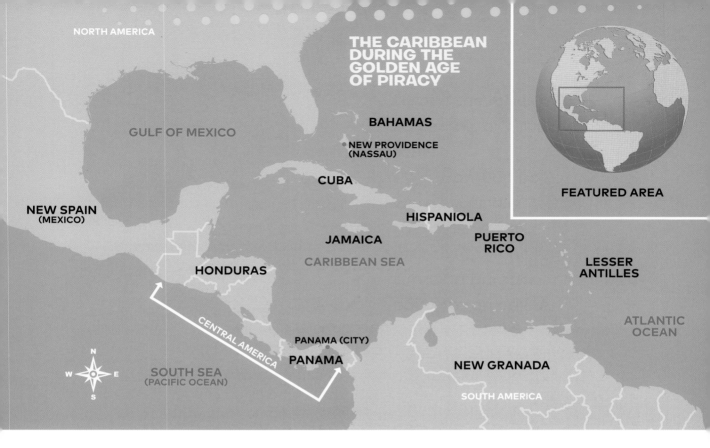

NORTH AMERICA

GULF OF MEXICO

BAHAMAS

NEW PROVIDENCE
(NASSAU)

CUBA

NEW SPAIN
(MEXICO)

HISPANIOLA

JAMAICA

PUERTO
RICO

CARIBBEAN SEA

HONDURAS

LESSER
ANTILLES

CENTRAL AMERICA

PANAMA (CITY)

PANAMA

ATLANTIC
OCEAN

SOUTH SEA
(PACIFIC OCEAN)

NEW GRANADA

SOUTH AMERICA

FEATURED AREA

some regions today. But the most famous era of piracy took place in the Caribbean Sea from the mid-1600s to the early 1700s.

This period is known as the Golden Age of Piracy. During this time, trade flourished between North America, South America, Europe, and Africa. The Caribbean Sea and surrounding waters were thick with pirates. These ocean **outlaws** were ready to prey on ships loaded with riches.

Timeline

1492 Explorer Christopher Columbus crosses the Atlantic Ocean, arriving in the Caribbean.

1668–1670 **Privateer** Henry Morgan and his crew conduct **raids** of Spanish settlements throughout Central America.
The Golden Age of Piracy begins.

1701–1714 England, France, and the Netherlands are at war over territory in Europe and North America.

1717 Pirate Edward "Blackbeard" Teach captures a French ship and renames it. He soon becomes one of the most feared pirates in North America.

1718 England's King George I pardons any pirate who **renounces** piracy. Many pirates accept his offer, and the Golden Age of Piracy ends soon after.

1807 Cheng I Sao takes over her husband's **fleet**, becoming one of the most successful pirate captains in history.

2009 The *Maersk Alabama* is captured by Somali pirates.

The Pirate Queen

One of the most successful pirates in history operated far away from the Caribbean. Cheng I Sao (also called Ching Shih) was from China. Cheng had married a pirate captain in 1801. The couple ruled a **fleet** of pirates in the South China Sea. When Cheng's husband died in 1807, Cheng took over the fleet.

Under Cheng's leadership, the fleet grew to more than 1,500 ships and 80,000 sailors. Then, in 1810, the Chinese government offered Cheng a deal. If Cheng ended her pirate ways, they would pardon her. Cheng agreed. She also got pardons for most of her men. Cheng retired from piracy and later died in 1844.

9

CHAPTER 2

History of Piracy

The first records of piracy date back more than 3,000 years. Ancient pirates attacked Greek trading ships in the Mediterranean Sea. When Romans came to power in Europe in the first century BCE, their ships were also attacked by pirates. Around the 800s CE, **Vikings** terrorized ships and settlements with their piracy.

Then, in 1492, Italian explorer Christopher Columbus crossed the Atlantic Ocean. Columbus arrived in the Caribbean, claiming the islands for Spain. Columbus was one of the first European explorers to cross the Atlantic Ocean. His journey marked the beginning of a period of exploration and piracy in the **New World**.

Before long, other Spanish ships were bound for the New World. These explorers built settlements in North, South, and Central America. They captured, killed, or enslaved the **indigenous** people living there. The explorers built mines and started plantations.

Hotshot Fact

Christopher Columbus arrived in what is now the Bahamas!

Other countries wanted to end Spain's **monopoly** on trade with the **New World**. These countries included England, France, and the Netherlands. These governments began hiring ships to attack Spanish trading ships. The

ships' captains obtained a **letter of marque** from their sponsoring government. This letter gave captains permission to attack and rob trading ships from other countries. These men became known as **privateers**. They were often former soldiers, sailors who had deserted their ships, and other laborers.

Privateering was considered legal, as long as the privateer had a letter of marque! The practice was made illegal by most European countries in 1856.

CHAPTER 3

Sea Outlaws

Henry Morgan was one of the most famous **privateers**. Historians believe he may have been part of a crew of privateers that captured Jamaica from the Spanish in 1655. Morgan and his crew were supported by England. They made Jamaica an English colony, and it quickly became a **haven** for privateers traveling in the Caribbean.

Morgan was elected captain of his crew. From 1668 to 1670, Morgan and his crew **raided** several Central American cities controlled by Spain. In 1671, they plundered the city of Panama. Spain was so angered by this raid that England decided to arrest Morgan and bring him to England to keep the peace. But once there, England's King Charles II changed his mind. He made Morgan a knight and the lieutenant governor of Jamaica.

England soon became involved in other conflicts. From 1702 to 1713, England and France were at war over control of North

Hotshot Fact

Panama was rebuilt 5 miles (8 km) away from its ruins. It was later named Panama City.

Immediately after the Panama raid, Morgan deserted his crew so he could keep all the treasure they stole for himself!

America. From 1701 to 1714, England, France, and the Netherlands were also at war over Spanish territory in Europe. By 1714, both wars were over. Trade flourished in the region.

With the countries at peace, governments no longer supported **privateers**. Former soldiers were now without work. Many former privateers and soldiers turned to piracy. The next few years saw the rise of some of history's most famous pirates.

In the 1710s, pirates began frequenting the

Blackbeard was one of the most famous pirates in history. He captured more than 30 ships during his pirate career.

Bahamian island of New Providence between **raids**. This island became a **haven** for many pirates who are still legendary today. Edward Teach was one pirate who often visited New Providence.

Teach was active from 1716 to 1718. He was nicknamed Blackbeard, for his long black beard. In 1717, Blackbeard captured a French ship, which he renamed *Queen Anne's Revenge*. The ship was one of the largest in the Caribbean.

Blackbeard was almost unstoppable. He eventually had a **fleet** of four ships and a crew of more than 200. He attacked ships and settlements throughout the Caribbean and up the North American coast. Blackbeard was killed by the English Navy off the coast of North Carolina in 1718.

By this time, piracy in the Caribbean had gotten out of control. Pirates were threatening the colonies in the Americas. These **outlaws** disrupted peace and trade. So, in 1718, England's King George I offered a deal to pirates. Anyone who **renounced** piracy would be given a pardon. However, pirates who refused the king's deal would be hunted and killed. Many pirates accepted the king's pardon. While piracy never disappeared, its Golden Age was over.

CHAPTER 4

A Pirate's Life

A pirate's life was often a short one. But it was exciting! It could also be very financially rewarding. This made piracy an attractive option for many young men. Most pirate crews were made up of former sailors and soldiers.

When pirates attacked a merchant ship, they also gave the ship's crew the option of joining the pirates. This invitation was also given to captive Africans who were aboard slave ships the pirates took over. On a pirate ship, black men had the same rights as their white crewmates. It is estimated that at least one-third of pirates during the Golden Age were black.

Hotshot Fact

Pirates often wore earrings. Young pirates were given earrings after their first voyage. Earrings were believed to protect the wearer. The earrings could also be sold to pay for a dead pirate's funeral.

DEMOCRACY AT WORK

Many people were drawn to the pirate life because of equality. The captain of a ship was usually elected by his crew and could be replaced at any time. A pirate captain only had full authority during attacks

While pirates hoped for gold and silver, their most common loot was grain, molasses, and rum.

or battles. During peaceful times, decisions were made by the group. Any **loot** captured during **raids** was divided somewhat equally between the crew. The captain and a few high-ranking crew received extra shares.

PIRATE CODE

Most pirate crews operated under a pirate code. This was an agreement between a pirate ship's captain and his crew. Pirate captain Bartholomew "Black Bart" Roberts developed a world-famous pirate code.

Roberts was one of the most successful Caribbean pirates. He was active between 1719 and 1722. During that time, he captured 400 ships! Roberts had a code that banned desertion, gambling, and stealing among his crew. It required lights out after 8:00 p.m. The code also listed how a pirate would be **compensated** if he lost a limb during an attack. Other ships may have had similar codes. Some of these codes were strictly enforced!

WOMEN PIRATES

Nearly all the pirates operating in the Caribbean were male. Many pirate captains, including Blackbeard, even refused to let women aboard their ships. They believed women were bad luck. Not all captains were so picky though.

Anne Bonny and Mary Read were two famous female pirates. They sailed under Captain John Rackham, who was

Black Bart commanded four ships and 500 pirates at the height of his career!

nicknamed Calico Jack, around 1720. The women were said to be as fierce as any men on the ship! After their ship was captured, Read died in jail, but Bonny was released.

CHAPTER 5

Ships

A pirate captain's ship was the most essential part of his operation. Pirates traveled on ships of all shapes and sizes. They usually relied on ships stolen during **raids**. Most pirates sailed on small, fast ships called sloops. These ships were often faster than the large merchant vessels pirates often attacked. Sloops could aid in a quick escape if an attack wasn't going well.

Sloops were also shallow enough to get near shore. Most sloops had a single mast and large sails. They could carry a crew of about 75. The ships could also carry 14 small cannons. Later pirates used American versions of sloops, called schooners. These could carry the same size crew as sloops but only held eight cannons.

Most merchants traveled on larger ships called

The skull and crossbones is the most famous pirate flag. However, many pirates used solid-colored flags or different designs.

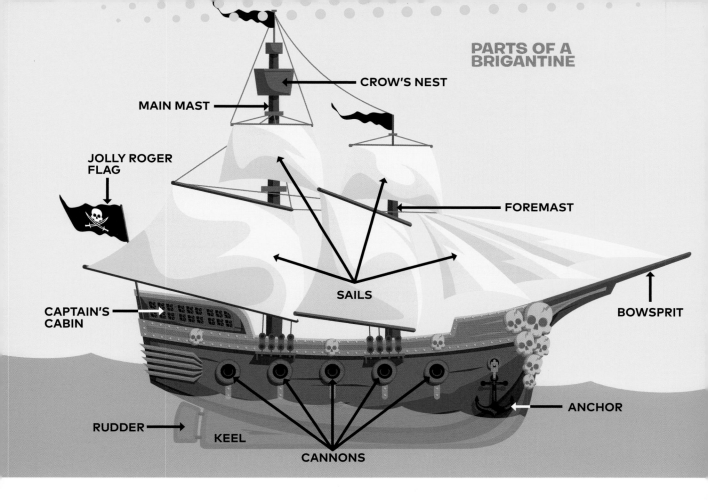

CROW'S NEST

MAIN MAST

JOLLY ROGER
FLAG

FOREMAST

SAILS

CAPTAIN'S
CABIN

BOWSPRIT

RUDDER

KEEL

CANNONS

ANCHOR

brigantines. These ships had two masts. They could carry a crew of 100 and 12 cannons. Frigates were warships, but they were often used for trading as well. They had three masts and could carry more than 40 cannons. These ships were slower, but some pirates preferred their firepower and storage space to sloops.

CHAPTER 6

Fearsome Pirates

A ship's cannons were a good advantage for pirates. But most pirates preferred to use cannons as little as possible. Cannon fire could permanently **damage** or even sink a ship. Instead, pirates hoped to capture the ship intact. They would get close enough to the ship to fire a warning shot. This would often cause the ship's captain and crew to surrender.

Pirates used other methods to inspire their victims to surrender. Blackbeard stuffed burning fuses under his hat, making it appear as if he were on fire. At more than six feet (1.8 m) tall, he was a terrifying sight. Pirate captains also created their own flags, called Jolly Rogers. The flags were usually black and often featured skeletons, skulls, or other frightening images.

Pirates weren't all show, however. Some pirates were known to torture and murder their victims. Stories of these cruel acts spread far and wide, inspiring greater fear of pirates. Despite these stories, most pirates didn't kill their victims. Pirates were after the ship and its goods. If the crew surrendered, the pirates might release them.

Most pirate ships were packed with 100 or more pirates. This was a method used to scare much smaller merchant crews.

Weapons

Pirates hoped their victims would surrender without a shot fired. But if their target resisted, the pirates were more than ready for a fight. Pirates would board the ship and fight hand-to-hand. Pirates were often better fighters and outnumbered merchant crews, so these **outlaws** usually won.

Pirates were well-armed and fierce fighters. Most pirates carried a musket, a pistol, and a cutlass. Muskets were long rifles. They were best for shooting long distances. Pistols were smaller guns that were used for short-range shooting. Cutlasses were short swords. They could cut through ropes, canvas sails, and even wood. Cutlasses were compact and lightweight, which made them ideal for combat in close quarters.

Some pirates also used bomb-like weapons called grenadoes. These were small balls filled with explosives. Pirates would light a grenado's fuse and throw the weapon toward a ship. Stinkpots were another weapon pirates used. These were pots filled with chemicals or other smelly items. Pirates would set the stinkpots on fire and toss them onto an

Muskets and pistols allowed pirates to attack enemies from a distance. However,
these weapons were difficult to use if they got wet!

enemy ship. The terrible smell distracted the enemy crew and
could even make them sick.

CHAPTER 8

Piracy Today

By the mid-1800s, piracy had greatly decreased around the world. But the practice still exists in modern times. In 2003, there were 445 attacks by pirates around the world. Most pirate attacks today take place off the coasts of Indonesia, Somalia, and Southeast Asia. Modern pirates use speedboats and machine guns. These **outlaws** still use some similar methods to Golden Age pirates.

MODERN PIRATES

Like historic pirates, modern pirates often target large cargo ships. They sneak aboard a ship at night or while the ship is slowed. In addition to stealing money and electronics, modern pirates often hold the crew **hostage**. They demand a **ransom** for the safe return of the crew. Shipping and insurance companies often pay these ransoms.

In 2009, the US ship *Maersk Alabama* was captured by Somali pirates. The crew managed to

Hotshot Fact

In 2013, the story of the *Maersk Alabama* was made into a film called *Captain Phillips*, starring actor Tom Hanks.

The Maersk Alabama *lifeboat* (left) *was just 28 feet (8.5 m) long. It contained food and water, but it didn't have a toilet or air flow.*

recapture their ship. But the pirates escaped in a lifeboat. They took the ship's captain, Richard Phillips, with them as a **hostage**. Navy SEALs rescued Phillips, killing three of the four pirates.

Piracy in Pop Culture

Modern pirates still inspire fear in cargo ship crews. But the Golden Age of Caribbean piracy has captured imaginations around the world. Pirates have been the subjects of popular plays, books, and films since the 1700s.

In 2003, Disney released a movie called *Pirates of the Caribbean*. It stars actor Johnny Depp as the bold and **eccentric** pirate Captain Jack Sparrow. The film was an instant success, becoming the first of five in the series. While entertaining, these films aren't a correct portrayal of pirate life.

With fictional pirates capturing so much attention, many people wanted to learn more about the history of Caribbean pirates. In 1997, a search team discovered the wreck of Blackbeard's *Queen Anne's Revenge*. Archaeologists worked to recover historic items from the site. Visitors can view these items at the North Carolina Maritime Museum and other museums in the United States.

In 2007, an exhibition called Real Pirates began touring museums around the United States and Canada. The exhibit

Captain Jack Sparrow is one of the most popular pirate characters. His famous look is a common costume for Halloween, festivals, and other events.

explored stories of Caribbean pirates and allowed visitors to see goods from the pirate ship *Whydah*. Millions of visitors learned about the *Whydah* and its pirates. The exhibit's success proves that fascination with pirates is as strong as it's ever been!

Glossary

compensate – to make a payment to, especially for work done or to make up for a loss.

damage – to cause harm or ruin.

democracy – a governmental system in which the people vote on how to run their country.

eccentric – odd or unusual.

fleet – a group of ships under one command.

haven – a place offering safety or favorable conditions.

hoist – to raise into position.

hostage – a person captured by another person or group in order to make a deal with authorities.

indigenous – native to a certain place.

infest – to spread or exist in large numbers so as to cause trouble or harm.

letter of marque – a letter granted by a nation giving a person permission to capture another nation's ships.

loot – things that have been stolen.

monopoly – complete control over the entire supply of a product or a service.

New World – the continents of the western half of Earth.

outlaw – a person who has broken the law or is running from the law.

privateer – a person who has his or her country's permission to attack foreign ships. The act of attacking foreign ships is privateering.

raid – a surprise attack or to carry out a surprise attack.

ransom – money demanded for the release of someone or something held captive.

renounce – to refuse to follow, obey, or recognize something.

Viking – a member of a group of warrior explorers from Scandinavia.

Index